MACMILLAN GUIDED READERS

ELEMENTARY LEVEL

ROBERT LOUIS STEVENSON

Treasure Island

Retold by Stephen Colbourn

FILTON
COLLEGE
ESOL

ELEMENTARY LEVEL

Founding Editor: John Milne

Macmillan Guided Readers provide a choice of enjoyable reading material for all learners of English. The series comprises three categories: MODERNS, CLASSICS and ORIGINALS. Macmillan **Classics** are retold versions of internationally recognised literature, published at four levels of grading – Beginner, Elementary, Intermediate and Upper. At **Elementary Level**, the control of content and language has the following main features:

Information Control

Stories have straightforward plots and a restricted number of main characters. Information which is vital to the understanding of the story is clearly presented and repeated when necessary. Difficult allusion and metaphor are avoided and cultural backgrounds are made explicit.

Structure Control

Students will meet those grammatical features which they have already been taught in their elementary course of studies. Other grammatical features occasionally occur with which the students may not be so familiar, but their use is made clear through context and reinforcement. This ensures that the reading as well as being enjoyable provides a continual learning situation for the students. Sentences are kept short – a maximum of two clauses in nearly all cases – and within sentences there is a balance of simple adverbial and adjectival phrases. Great care is taken with pronoun reference.

Vocabulary Control

At **Elementary Level** there is a limited use of carefully controlled vocabulary of approximately 1100 basic words. At the same time, students are given some opportunity to meet new or unfamiliar words in contexts where their meaning is obvious. The meaning of words introduced in this way is reinforced by repetition. Help is also given to the students in the form of vivid illustrations which are closely related to the text.

Contents

Notes About This Story

The Author

Robert Louis Stevenson was born in Edinburgh, Scotland, in November 1850. *Treasure Island* is one of his most famous stories. His other stories include *Kidnapped, The Black Arrow, The Strange Case Of Dr Jekyll and Mr Hyde*, and *The Master of Ballantrae*.

Stevenson was ill for much of his life. He went to live in the South Pacific because the weather was warm there. He died in Samoa in December 1894.

The Book

The story takes place in the middle of the eighteenth century. It is the story of pirates who stole treasure from ships in the Caribbean. These pirates buried the treasure on an island. The pirates were cruel and violent. They all wanted the treasure. They fought and killed each other.

Treasure Island is not a true story. Captain Flint and Long John Silver were not real pirates. Treasure Island is not a real place. But there were pirates in many parts of the world in the eighteenth century.

There were pirates in the Mediterranean, the Caribbean and the China Seas. Ships went from South America to Spain. These ships carried gold, silver and goods across the Caribbean. And they were often attacked by pirates. The pirates killed the sailors and stole everything in the ships.

Some famous pirates were Captain Henry Morgan,

Blackbeard and Mary Read. They were cruel and violent people. Pirates were often hanged if they were caught.

People always enjoy stories about pirates. There are many books and films about pirates. Some of the stories are true and some of them are not true. All of them are exciting! *Treasure Island* is one of the most famous stories.

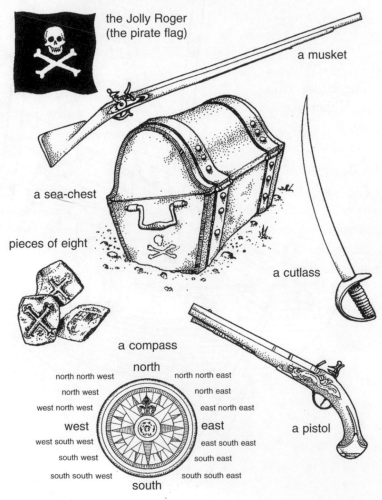

the Jolly Roger
(the pirate flag)

a musket

a sea-chest

pieces of eight

a cutlass

a compass

north

north north west   north north east

north west   north east

west north west   east north east

west   east   a pistol

west south west   east south east

south west   south east

south south west   south south east

south

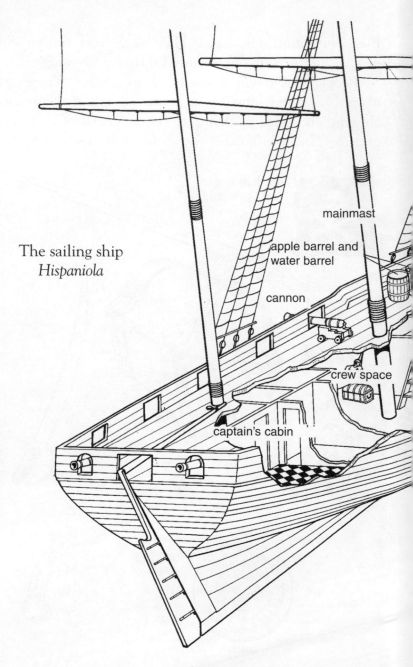

The sailing ship
Hispaniola

mainmast

apple barrel and
water barrel

cannon

crew space

captain's cabin

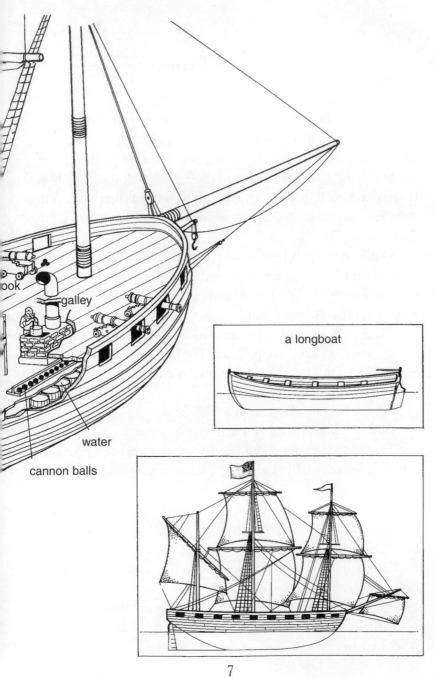

ook

galley

a longboat

water

cannon balls

1

The Old Pirate

My name is Jim Hawkins. I am going to tell you a story about pirates and treasure. This story started a long time ago, in the year 1756, when I was twelve years old.

My father owned an inn called The Admiral Benbow. It was a small inn on the south coast of England. The Admiral Benbow was not very busy. We did not get many customers.

Sometimes travellers stayed at the inn. They could buy a meal and have something to drink. They usually stayed for only one night. But I remember one traveller who stayed at The Admiral Benbow for several weeks.

I remember the day he arrived. A horse and cart came along the road and stopped outside the inn. An old sailor got down from the cart and came to the inn door. He was singing a sailor's song.

Fifteen men on the dead man's chest –
Yo-ho-ho and a bottle of rum!

The old sailor knocked loudly on the inn door and my father opened it. I stood next to my father and looked at the sailor.

The man was tall and his face was brown from the sun. His hair was white. It was tied in a tail at the back of his head. He wore an old blue coat.

'Bring me a glass of rum,' the sailor said loudly to my father.

I looked at the horse and cart. There was a wooden box on the cart – the sailor's wooden chest. It was big and it looked heavy.

'Do many people stay here?' the sailor asked my father.

'Not many,' my father replied. 'We always have empty rooms.'

'Good. I will stay here,' said the sailor. 'I will stay here for several weeks.' He took some money out of his pocket. 'Take this money. Tell me when I have spent it all.'

He gave my father four gold coins.

'Thank you, sir,' said my father. 'May I ask your name?'

'Call me Captain,' said the sailor. 'Now, bring my chest and show me my room.'

My father carried the heavy wooden chest into the inn. He carried it to the Captain's room. I did not know what was in the chest, but it looked very heavy.

The Captain stayed for several weeks. I was afraid of him. He drank bottles of rum and he was drunk every day. He sang songs and shouted loudly when he was drunk.

'Boy!' he shouted. 'Bring me more rum!'

When I had brought the rum he told me stories. He told stories about pirates and ships. He told me about robbing ships and killing men. Then he sang sailors' songs.

'Jim,' the Captain often said to me, 'Jim – look out for a man with one leg. Watch for a man with one leg. Tell me if you see him. Do this and I'll pay you well.'

I said nothing. I was too afraid to speak. Who was this man with one leg?

———

Winter came and my father fell sick. He was very ill and the doctor came to see him every day. The doctor's name was Dr Livesey. He said my father did not have long to live.

My mother and I were very busy. We had to look after

the inn while my father lay ill in bed. But my father did not get much rest. The Captain drank rum and sang and shouted.

'Please be quiet,' Dr Livesey said to the Captain. 'There is a very sick man upstairs.'

'What?' shouted the Captain. 'What did you say? No one tells me what to do!' He pulled a knife out of the pocket of his coat.

'Put that knife down at once,' Dr Livesey said. He stared hard at the Captain. 'Put that knife down. Or I will call the soldiers to arrest you.'

The Captain stared at Dr Livesey, but he put down the knife. He drank another glass of rum.

'And if you drink rum every day, you will soon be dead,' the doctor went on.

The Captain was quiet for several days.

———

Dr Livesey was visiting my father one morning when a stranger came to the inn. The Doctor was upstairs with my father and mother. I was alone downstairs, in the main room of the inn.

The stranger opened the front door and looked at me. I did not like the man. He was dirty and had a ragged beard. His face was hard and cruel.

'Where's Captain Bill?' he asked.

'I don't know Captain Bill,' I replied. I did not want to tell the man anything.

'I know he's staying here,' said the stranger. 'I want to talk to him.'

The Captain came into the room. He did not know the stranger was there.

'Hello, Billy,' said the stranger.

'Black Dog!' said the Captain. His face went white. 'What do you want?'

'We must talk,' said Black Dog to the Captain. Then the stranger shouted to me, 'Get us some rum, boy.'

I went into the kitchen to get some rum. The Captain and Black Dog were talking. Suddenly they started to shout.

I went back into the room. The Captain had a short, heavy sword called a cutlass. He raised the cutlass and ran towards Black Dog. Black Dog ran out of the inn. The Captain chased him and swung his cutlass at Black Dog's head. But the Captain didn't hit him. The cutlass hit the wooden sign above the inn door. Black Dog escaped and ran down the road.

The Captain stopped running and turned round. His face was a terrible purple colour. He stepped back into the inn and fell on the floor.

'Dr Livesey!' I called. 'Dr Livesey! Help!'

Dr Livesey came downstairs from my father's room. He looked closely at the Captain.

'I said that rum is going to kill him,' Dr Livesey said. 'We must put him to bed. Let him sleep.'

I helped the Doctor to put the Captain into his bed. We now had two sick men in the house and I looked after them both. But soon there was only one sick man because my father died suddenly one night.

*The Captain chased Black Dog and swung his cutlass
at Black Dog's head.*

2

The Black Spot

Dr Livesey was very kind. He helped us make arrangements for my father's funeral.

The Captain did not leave his bed for many days. He did not get up until after the funeral. When he got up he started to drink rum.

'I must get away from here, Jim,' the Captain said to me. 'Tell Dr Livesey. Tell him I was a pirate. Tell him I sailed on Captain Flint's ship.'

I had heard of Captain Flint. Sailors told stories about him. Captain Flint had been a terrible pirate. He had killed many men and robbed many ships.

'Flint's men want to find me,' the Captain went on. 'I was on Flint's ship with them. Now they want the chest. They want the sea-chest in my room. I must get away.'

But the Captain could not go anywhere. He was too drunk.

I heard a noise outside the inn. It was the noise of someone tapping a stick on the road. The noise came closer and closer. Then I heard a voice calling, 'Will anyone help me?'

I looked outside and saw a beggar standing in the road. He was dressed in ragged clothes and wore a green cloth over his eyes. He was blind. He tapped a stick in front of him as he walked.

'Will anyone help a poor blind man?' shouted the beggar, 'Will anyone tell me where I am?'

'You are at The Admiral Benbow Inn,' I said.

'I hear a young voice, a kind voice,' said the beggar.

'Will you hold my hand, young sir?'

I held out my hand to the beggar and he took hold of it. But the blind man suddenly pulled me towards him and twisted my arm.

'Now, boy, take me to the Captain,' said the beggar. 'Take me to the Captain or I'll break your arm.'

He twisted my arm again and I cried out. I was very frightened, but I took him to the Captain.

I thought that the Captain would be angry. I thought that he would shout. But the Captain said nothing. He sat at a table with a bottle of rum in front of him. His face was white.

'Blind Pew!' said the Captain. 'You've come at last.'

'Aye, Captain, I've come,' said Pew, the blind beggar. 'Now, boy,' Pew said to me, 'hold out the Captain's left hand.'

I did as I was told. I took hold of the Captain's left hand and held it out to Blind Pew. Blind Pew put a piece of paper in the Captain's hand. There was a large black spot on the paper.

'The Black Spot!' shouted the Captain. The colour of his face changed from white to red.

'Aye, Captain, it's the Black Spot,' said Blind Pew. 'Now you know. We'll come for you tonight.'

Blind Pew let go of my arm and walked to the door. He held his stick out in front of him. He left the inn and I heard his stick tap on the road.

The Captain stood up. He put his hand on his throat. His face was purple.

'The chest, Jim! Get my sea-chest!'

The Captain fell down onto the floor.

'Mother!' I called.

Blind Pew put a piece of paper in the Captain's hand. There was a large black spot on the paper.

We both tried to help the Captain, but he was dead.

Quickly I told my mother what had happened. 'Men are coming,' I said. 'Men – pirates – I don't know. They want the Captain's sea-chest.'

'We must get help,' said my mother. 'We must get help from the village.'

My mother and I ran outside. We ran to the village. We told people there was trouble at The Admiral Benbow. We told them that pirates were coming.

But no one wanted to help us. Everyone was afraid. At last one man sent his son to get Dr Livesey.

'Dr Livesey will know what to do,' said the man.

It was dark when my mother and I returned to The Admiral Benbow. We were alone and afraid.

I lit a candle. There, on the floor, lay the body of the Captain. The Black Spot lay in his hand.

'Let's open his sea-chest,' I said.

We went to the Captain's room to find the sea-chest. The wooden box was locked. I had to look in the dead man's pockets for a key.

The Captain's face was purple and black. His eyes were open. His body was cold. I found a key on a chain round his neck.

We opened the wooden chest with the key. Inside the chest was a bag of money and a leather packet. My mother started to count the money.

'I'll take the money he owes me and no more,' she said.

But there were many coins. Some coins were English pounds. Some coins were Spanish pieces of eight.

I heard a noise outside. I heard a whistle.

'Hurry!' I said. 'Hurry. The pirates are coming.'

But my mother kept counting the gold coins.

Outside I heard the tap-tap, tap-tap of a stick. I knew Blind Pew had come back.

'Leave the money and run!' I said. 'The pirates will kill us.'

I took the leather packet from the chest. My mother took a few coins. We opened the back door and ran out of the inn. We ran towards the village.

Behind us we heard shouts. Men were outside the inn. They kicked open the front door. Then I heard the voice of Blind Pew.

'Get the chest! Get the map!' Blind Pew shouted.

Suddenly we heard another sound. My mother and I stopped running. We could not see the road because the night was dark. But we heard the sound of horses. We heard many men riding horses towards us. Then we heard the sound of a gunshot. A pistol was fired in the darkness.

'Run!' a voice shouted.

'Don't leave me!' shouted Blind Pew.

My mother and I went back towards the inn. Lights were burning in the windows. We saw men running towards the sea. Blind Pew ran along the road tapping his stick. The sound of the horses on the road was getting louder.

'Don't leave me!' Blind Pew shouted. He tried to run after his friends. But the road was rough and he fell to the ground.

The horsemen did not see Blind Pew in the darkness. They rode over him. Blind Pew gave a terrible scream. I knew he was dead.

3

The Captain's Papers

The horsemen were Customs men. Customs men guarded the coast around Britain. They tried to catch anyone who broke the law. Dr Livesey had received our message and he had brought the Customs men to the inn.

There was a man called Squire Trelawney with Dr Livesey. Squire John Trelawney was rich. He lived in a big white house on the hill outside the village. Dr Livesey and Squire Trelawney asked us many questions.

'What did the pirates want?' asked Dr Livesey. 'Did they want money?'

'The old Captain had some money,' I said. 'But they were looking for something else. I think they wanted this leather packet.'

I showed them the leather packet from the Captain's sea-chest. Dr Livesey opened the packet. There were papers inside.

'These papers belonged to Captain Flint, the pirate,' said Squire Trelawney. He pointed at one of the papers.

'Look. Here is his name.'

'Was the dead Captain called Captain Flint?' I asked.

'No, no,' said Squire Trelawney. 'The dead man here is not Captain Flint. Captain Flint died in South America. He was a terrible pirate. For twenty years he robbed ships and killed men. He was a rich man when he died. But no one knows what happened to all his money.'

A thick piece of paper fell out of the leather packet. Dr Livesey picked it up.

'Look at this,' said Dr Livesey. 'It's a map.'

Captain Flint's Map

Squire Trelawney took the paper and put it on the table. It was a map of an island. Some instructions were written on the map. There was also a red cross drawn on the map. Over the cross, in red letters, was written "Flint's Treasure".

'This map shows us where Flint buried his treasure,' said Squire Trelawney. 'The letters tell us how to get to the island. We're the only ones who know the secret now.'

'But other men know about the map,' said Dr Livesey. 'The men who came to the inn tonight – the pirates – they were looking for the map.'

'I am a rich man,' said Squire Trelawney. 'I will go to Bristol. I will pay for the use of a ship. There are many ships in Bristol. A ship will be ready in three weeks. We will sail to this island and find the treasure. We will dig it up.'

I looked at Squire Trelawney. I did not think he wanted me to go with him, but I was wrong.

'Dr Livesey,' said Squire Trelawney, 'you will be the ship's doctor. And Jim Hawkins will be the cabin boy.'

4
Long John Silver

Squire Trelawney spoke to my mother. He said he wanted me to go with him on a sea voyage. He arranged for a boy to work at the Admiral Benbow while I was away. Then Squire Trelawney went to Bristol to charter a ship.

I was very excited. I wanted to sail to Treasure Island.

At last, Dr Livesey received a letter from Squire Trelawney in Bristol.

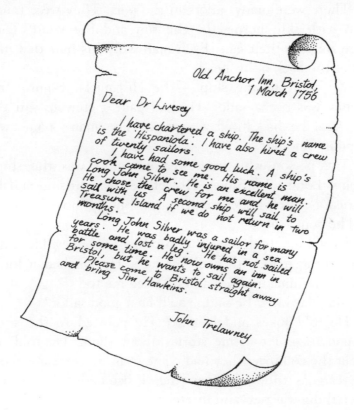

Old Anchor Inn, Bristol,
1 March 1756

Dear Dr Livesey

I have chartered a ship. The ship's name is the 'Hispaniola'. I have also hired a crew of twenty sailors.

I have had some good luck. A ship's cook came to see me. His name is Long John Silver. He is an excellent man. He chose the crew for me and he will sail with us. A second ship will sail to Treasure Island if we do not return in two months.

Long John Silver was a sailor for many years. He was badly injured in a sea battle and lost a leg. He has not sailed for some time. He now owns an inn in Bristol, but he wants to sail again. Please come to Bristol straight away and bring Jim Hawkins.

John Trelawney

Dr Livesey came to The Admiral Benbow and I said goodbye to my mother. Then the Doctor took me to Bristol.

We travelled in a coach pulled by horses. It was a long journey and I had never travelled so far before. I had never seen a city.

We arrived at the port of Bristol early in the morning. The port was very busy. It was full of ships. Ships sailed to and from every part of the world. All day and all night men loaded and unloaded all kinds of cargo from the ships.

There were many sailors in the port. They were tough men with skin burned by the sun and the wind. They wore rings in their ears. Each man wore his hair tied in a tail at the back of his head.

We went to the ship – the *Hispaniola*. Squire Trelawney was not a sailor. He had paid a crew to sail the ship and he had hired a captain. The man's name was Captain Smollett.

The person who interested me most was the ship's cook – Long John Silver. His left leg was missing and he carried a crutch under his left arm. But he moved quickly and he could run.

I saw him climb onto the ship like a monkey. He was a tall, strong man with a clever face. He laughed a lot. I liked him immediately – and he liked me too.

'Jim Hawkins,' he said, 'you'll be a good sailor.'

He told jokes and laughed. He pointed to the ships around us and told me stories about them. He told me about the countries they had come from. He told me about the cargoes they were carrying. I listened and learned. Everything was new and interesting.

Long John Silver pointed to the ships around us and told me stories about them. I listened and learned.

The rest of the crew came aboard the ship. The next morning, we sailed away from Bristol and I was kept busy in the galley.

I was the ship's cabin boy. So I worked with Long John Silver in the galley. The galley was the ship's kitchen. I helped to cook and carry the food to the crew. After their meals, I cleared away the plates and washed them.

At the end of each day I was very tired. I did not sleep in a bed – I slept in a hammock. The hammock hung between two wooden posts. The hammock moved as the ship moved, from side to side, and it was very comfortable.

Captain Smollett came to look at the galley. Silver was polite and helpful. Captain Smollett looked hard at Long John Silver. But he did not say anything.

Long John Silver kept a parrot. This bird lived in a cage in the galley. Silver had taught it to speak.

'The parrot's name is Captain Flint,' said Silver.

'Pieces of eight! Pieces of eight!' said the parrot, over and over again.

I was happy at sea. We sailed west into the Atlantic Ocean. There was some bad weather for a few days. Then the wind and rain disappeared and the weather became warmer.

Every day Captain Smollett wrote in the ship's log. He wrote about our journey and about what was happening on the ship.

The crew seemed quite happy. They ate their food. They sang songs and told stories and the days passed quickly. Long John Silver cooked the men's food. The men ate the food and never complained. They seemed afraid of Silver.

5

The Apple Barrel

There were two tall wooden barrels on deck. One of the barrels had fresh water inside. There were apples inside the other barrel. The men could take apples and water whenever they wanted to.

We had been at sea for a month. The apple barrel was nearly empty. I climbed into the barrel because I could not see the bottom of it. There were only one or two apples left. I started to eat one while I was inside the barrel.

It was almost dark and I had finished work. The inside of the barrel was warm. The darkness and the movement of the ship made me sleepy. I fell asleep for a few minutes.

I woke up when I heard voices. Two men were standing by the barrel and talking. One voice belonged to Long John Silver. The other voice was a young sailor's. They did not know I was in the barrel.

'I sailed with Flint,' said Silver. 'I was fighting for Flint when I lost my leg. A cannon shot blew my leg off. The same cannon shot made Pew blind. Most of the men aboard this ship sailed with Flint too. I hired the crew. They know me – they are my shipmates.'

'How long will you wait, Silver?' asked the other voice. 'When will we take over the ship?'

'I'm not in a hurry,' said Silver. 'Let the Squire and his friends take us to the island. They've got the map. Let them find the treasure – Flint's treasure.'

'And after that?'

'We'll kill them all,' said Long John Silver. 'Dead men tell no tales.'

Two men were standing by the barrel and talking.
They did not know I was in the barrel.

Their conversation stopped. The look-out at the top of the mast shouted, 'Land-ho! I see land!'

The crew ran onto the deck and stared across the sea. While they were looking towards the land, I got out of the barrel. I suddenly felt very afraid of Long John Silver.

I looked across the sea. There was an island to the south. We could see it in the bright moonlight.

Captain Smollett talked to Squire Trelawney and Dr Livesey. Then he spoke the crew.

'Men,' said Captain Smollett, 'this is the island we have been looking for. Tonight you can drink some rum.'

The men were happy and they cheered. The Captain went to his cabin with Squire Trelawney and Dr Livesey. I followed them and knocked on the cabin door.

'Sir, I have something to tell you,' I said to Squire Trelawney. Then I told them what Long John Silver had said.

Squire Trelawney looked surprised. I do not think he believed me. Captain Smollett was not surprised. He believed me immediately.

'So,' said Captain Smollett, 'we have a crew of pirates. Silver is a pirate who sailed with Flint. Silver hired this crew. They are waiting to take over the ship. They will try to murder us. How many men will help us?'

'I brought three of my servants with me,' said Squire Trelawney. 'There are four of us in this cabin. That makes seven of us against nineteen pirates. We must make careful plans.'

6

Murder

The next morning the *Hispaniola* stopped in a bay. The ship was anchored close to the shore and Captain Smollett looked at the island through a telescope. He also looked at the treasure map.

I had seen the map. I knew the tall hill on the island was called Spy-Glass Hill. I knew that there was an old wooden building called a stockade near the shore. But I could not see the stockade when I looked at the island. Sailors had built the stockade many years ago while they repaired their ship.

All morning the men were restless. They did not obey the Captain's orders quickly. Captain Smollett watched the crew carefully. Only Long John Silver was happy.

'I'll let some men go ashore this afternoon,' said Captain Smollett. 'I'll fire a gun half an hour before sundown. That will be the time to return.'

The Captain waited to see how many men wanted to go ashore. He wanted to see how many men would go with Silver. And he wanted to see how many men would stay with Livesey, Trelawney and himself. Many of the men wanted to go with Silver. They thought that they would find the treasure on the island immediately. They wanted to go ashore at once.

I wanted to go ashore too. I knew it was dangerous. But I had been at sea for a month. I wanted to feel the land under my feet.

I did not tell Dr Livesey and Squire Trelawney that I was going. I climbed into one of the small boats with the men. There were six men in one boat and seven in the other. Silver was in the other boat. He was feeding his parrot.

'Pieces of eight! Pieces of eight!' the parrot screamed.

Long John Silver did not see me until we were close to the shore.

'Jim, Jim!' I heard Silver call. 'Stay with me on the island, Jim.'

But I didn't listen. I jumped out of the boat and ran up the beach. I ran straight ahead. There were trees in front of me. I ran through the trees and the thick bushes.

There were strange flowers and plants everywhere. There were brightly coloured birds and insects. Sometimes I could see Spy-Glass Hill above the trees. Most of the time the trees hid the sky. I walked and walked. I did not know where I was going. I was lost in the jungle.

I must have walked in a circle because I heard voices ahead of me. I heard Long John Silver's voice. I moved forward slowly and hid in the trees.

'Join us, Tom,' Silver was saying to another man. 'All the crew are working together in this. You will be alone.'

'I'll not join you,' said Tom. 'I'll not join a crew of pirates. We're not all thieves and murderers like you. I'm not alone.'

Just then there was a scream. A man gave a terrible cry and frightened birds flew up into the air.

'What was that?' asked Tom.

'That was Alan,' said Silver. 'Alan didn't want to join us either.'

'And you've killed him,' said Tom. He was angry and afraid. 'You've killed him like a dog. And you'll have to kill me too, if you can.'

'I'll not join you,' said Tom. 'I'll not join a crew of pirates.'

Tom turned and walked away from Long John Silver.

Silver was quick. He leant against a tree. He lifted his crutch and threw it at Tom like a spear. The crutch hit the man in the back. Tom fell down.

Quickly, Silver jumped forwards on his one leg. A knife was in his hand. He jumped on Tom. He stabbed the knife into Tom's back. Once. Twice. Tom did not move again.

I was horrified. I had seen a murder. I could not move. I had liked Long John Silver. Now I had seen him kill a man.

7

The Man on the Island

After a few moments I turned and ran away. I had to get away from the dead man and the murderer.

Then I stopped running. Once again I was afraid. I knew I was not alone. There was someone else in the trees. It was a man – the strangest man I had ever seen. I stared at him.

The man came towards me slowly. He had long white hair and a long beard. His clothes were torn and ragged. He wore a leather belt round his waist.

'Who are you?' I asked quietly. I was ready to run away from this strange man.

'I'm Ben Gunn,' the man replied, 'and I haven't spoken to a man for three years. I was marooned.'

Marooned! Left alone to die on this island! I had heard that pirates sometimes marooned men on islands.

'I'm Ben Gunn,' the man said, 'and I haven't spoken to a
man for three years. I was marooned.'

'You're still alive!' I said. 'How have you managed to live?'

'I eat fruit and catch fish,' said Ben Gunn. 'And every night I dream of eating cheese. But tell me – what's your name?'

'Jim,' I said.

'And who's with you?'

'No one,' I replied, 'but I was with a man called Long John Silver a short time ago.'

'Long John Silver!' said Ben Gunn. 'I know Silver. We were on Flint's ship together. Flint buried his treasure on this island.'

'Yes, I know,' I said.

'They left me here.'

'Who left you here?' I asked. 'Why did they leave you?'

'Flint's men left me here,' he said. 'After Flint died we came back to the island. Flint's men wanted to find the treasure. I said I knew where the treasure was. But I didn't know. So they marooned me here.'

Ben Gunn's eyes were bright and staring. He looked mad.

'Now, will you take me home?' asked Ben Gunn. 'I'll make you rich. And I've got a boat. It's here. I'll show you. I'll show you my boat.'

I looked towards the place where Ben Gunn was pointing. But I did not go to the boat. Suddenly there was the loud sound of a cannon shot. It was still two hours before sundown. This was not the captain's signal to return to the *Hispaniola*. Why was the cannon firing? Now there was the sound of more shooting.

'The pirates have begun to fight,' I said. And I ran back through the jungle towards the noise.

8

The Stockade

Dr Livesey Continues the Story

I am Dr Livesey. I am writing this part of the story. I am writing about what happened when Jim Hawkins went to the island on his own.

Thirteen men went ashore in two boats. I stayed on the *Hispaniola* with Captain Smollett and Squire Trelawney. I saw the boats reach the shore. I saw Jim Hawkins run into the trees on the island. I was surprised. He had not told us where he was going.

The Captain and I looked at the treasure map again. The map showed a small wooden stockade on the island. I told Captain Smollett and Squire Trelawney that I had a plan.

'Let us take guns and food to the stockade,' I said. 'We will be safer on the island than on the ship. Also, there is water to drink in the stockade.'

'Yes, let us go to the island,' said Squire Trelawney. 'Long John Silver is on the island with twelve men. There are six of his men on the ship. If we wait, they will all attack us here. We will be safer in the stockade on the island.'

We began to load food, muskets and pistols into a small boat. The ship had three boats. Silver and his men had taken two of them. We used the third one. There were six of us – Squire Trelawney, his three servants, Captain Smollett and me.

Silver's men stayed on board the *Hispaniola*. The six

men watched us as we got ready to leave.

Captain Smollett and I each had two pistols. Silver's men moved towards us.

'Stay back,' I said. I pointed my pistols at them. 'Keep away.'

The six men watched us as we loaded the small boat. They did not know what to do. They did not come near us. They watched.

When the boat was full, Captain Smollett told us to get in. Squire Trelawney got in the boat. Then his three servants followed him and so did I.

Captain Smollett spoke to Silver's men left on the ship. 'We are leaving the *Hispaniola*,' he said. 'Do any of you want to join us?'

After a moment, one of the six men moved forward. 'I'll join you,' he said. 'I'm not a pirate.'

The pirate next to him had a knife. There was a short fight, but the man got into our boat. He had a deep cut on his cheek and blood ran down his face.

We pushed the small boat away from the *Hispaniola*. Now there were seven of us in that small boat. We also carried food and guns. There was too much in the boat.

We rowed the boat slowly towards the shore.

'They're going to fire the cannon at us!' Captain Smollett shouted.

I looked back at the ship. The men on the *Hispaniola* were aiming the cannon at us.

'Give me a musket,' said Squire Trelawney. 'I'll shoot one of them.'

Squire Trelawney stood up in the boat. He aimed the long musket at the men on the ship. He fired.

One of the men on the ship cried out and fell down,

but the others aimed the cannon at us. When the cannon fired, we all tried to lie down in the boat. The shot from the cannon missed us. But our small boat moved dangerously from side to side.

Water came over the side of the boat. The little boat was so heavy that it sank.

'Save the guns! Save the gunpowder!' shouted Captain Smollett. 'Save as much as you can!'

The water was not deep and we were near the shore. So we walked to the island.

We carried the guns and the barrels of gunpowder high above our heads to keep them dry. Most of our food was lost, but we saved the guns.

'Go to the stockade!' shouted the Captain. 'Go to the stockade. Quickly!'

The wooden stockade was not far from the shore. It had a low wall around it. The wall was made from the trunks of trees. In the centre of the stockade there was a wooden cabin.

We had almost reached the gate of the stockade when seven men ran out of the jungle.

They were Silver's men – pirates. They had guns and cutlasses.

Squire Trelawney fired a pistol at the men. One of them fell. The others ran back into the jungle and fired their guns at us.

One of Squire Trelawney's men was hit in the chest and fell down. We pulled him into the stockade and closed the gate.

I looked at the man. He was dead.

The pirates on the ship fired the cannon at the stockade. They missed, but they made a lot of noise.

Squire Trelawney fired a pistol at the pirates. They ran back into the jungle and fired their guns at us.

Captain Smollett had brought the ship's log. He wrote down what had happened.

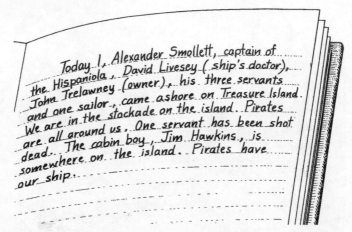

Today I, Alexander Smollett, captain of the Hispaniola, David Livesey (ship's doctor), John Trelawney (owner), his three servants and one sailor, came ashore on Treasure Island. We are in the stockade on the island. Pirates are all around us. One servant has been shot dead. The cabin boy, Jim Hawkins, is somewhere on the island. Pirates have our ship.

Suddenly I heard a shout outside. I looked out of the cabin and saw Jim Hawkins climbing over the wall of the stockade.

9

The Fight with the Pirates

Jim Hawkins Continues the Story

I left Ben Gunn as soon as I heard the cannon on the *Hispaniola* firing. I ran towards the sound of the guns firing from the stockade. I did not know where the stockade was, but I followed the noise.

The cannon fired again. A cannon ball landed in the jungle near me. I stopped running.

Ben Gunn ran up to me and held my arm. 'Your friends are in the stockade,' he said. 'I want to meet them. Bring them to me. I will help.'

Another cannon ball fell near us. We both ran away and Ben Gunn disappeared into the jungle.

For an hour, cannon balls crashed into the jungle. I slowly went towards the shore. I saw the *Hispaniola* firing its cannons at the stockade.

The *Hispaniola* had a new flag. The flag was the Jolly Roger – a black flag with a white skull and crossbones. It was the pirate flag!

At last the ship stopped firing its cannons. Quickly, I ran towards the stockade.

I shouted to the men inside – 'Don't shoot! It's Jim!' And I climbed the wooden wall.

Dr Livesey came out of the cabin to meet me. I told him my story. I told him about Ben Gunn. I told him that Ben Gunn wanted to help us.

'But I think he's mad, sir,' I said at the end of my tale.

'He was marooned on this island for three years,' said

Dr Livesey. 'I'm not surprised he's mad.'

At sundown we buried Squire Trelawney's servant in the sand. Then we slept. But each of us stayed awake for part of the night to watch for pirates.

I was woken by a voice calling- 'Don't fire! I have a flag of truce!' It was Long John Silver's voice.

Silver stood outside the stockade. He was leaning on his crutch and he carried a white flag in his hand.

Captain Smollett spoke to us. 'Don't fire,' he said. 'But don't come out of the cabin.' Then he walked to the gate of the stockade.

'What do you want, Silver?' Captain Smollett called out.

'I don't want to hurt you,' Long John Silver called back. 'I want the treasure. I want the treasure map.'

'You won't get it,' Captain Smollett shouted.

'Then you won't get out of this stockade alive,' said Silver. 'Give me the map and I'll let you live.'

'All I'll give you is one minute to get out of here,' shouted Captain Smollett. 'Then I'll start firing.'

'You'll be dead in an hour,' Silver shouted. Then he turned and went back into the jungle.

'Get ready for an attack,' Captain Smollett said. We loaded the muskets. We stood by the windows of the cabin. We did not have long to wait.

Soon musket shots cracked out from the jungle. The pirates fired on us from three sides. They fired over the low walls of the stockade. We kept our heads down.

Suddenly a group of seven men jumped over the low wall of the stockade and ran towards the cabin.

We fired our muskets at them. Two of the pirates were shot dead. A third pirate was wounded and fell to the ground. But four of them reached the cabin. They had cutlasses and pistols.

One of the men kicked open the cabin door. He swung his sharp cutlass at us. I jumped out of his way. A cutlass can cut off a man's head. Two more pirates came through the open door. Now there were three of them inside the cabin.

A pirate pulled a musket out of Dr Livesey's hands. He hit one of Squire Trelawney's servants on the side of the head. The poor man fell to the ground. Blood came from his nose and mouth.

I picked up a cutlass and started to fight. A pirate tried to hit my head but Captain Smollett killed him with his cutlass. The Squire shot another man with his pistol.

Dr Livesey ran outside. A pirate had climbed on the roof of the cabin. He was trying to fire at us from above. Dr Livesey swung a musket at the man's legs and knocked him off the roof.

There was smoke everywhere from the pistols and muskets. Men shouted and screamed.

Then suddenly the fight was over. I stood alone in the smoke. There was a strange silence. The pirates had run back to the jungle. We had won the first fight.

Another of Squire Trelawney's servants was dead. Captain Smollett was wounded. There were four of us left standing by the cabin. There were four dead pirates on the ground.

We waited, but the pirates did not come back that day. We made a meal and buried the dead men. By evening we felt safer. But we knew the pirates would come back. If we waited, they would attack us again and again.

Then I thought of a plan. It was a dangerous plan. I did not want to tell the others about it. I was sure they would think the plan was too dangerous.

I said nothing to the others. I waited until sundown. I put two pistols and a sharp knife in my belt. When it was dark, I climbed over the wall of the stockade. No one saw me leave.

10
Ben Gunn's Boat

I went back to the place where I had met Ben Gunn. He had pointed to the shore and said – 'I have a boat.' Now I wanted to find that boat.

The moon was shining brightly. I quickly went down to the shore. The *Hispaniola* was anchored out in the bay.

I was not afraid of the pirates. I could see and hear them. They had made a big fire on the beach. They were drinking rum and laughing. They were sitting by the fire.

Soon I found the place where Ben Gunn had hidden his boat. But Ben Gunn's boat was small. It was only big enough for one man. Inside the boat was a paddle.

I carried the boat down to the beach and put it in the water. I paddled the boat out into the bay. I paddled towards the *Hispaniola*.

Quietly I stopped beside the *Hispaniola*. I could hear voices. Men were laughing and joking. Were they drunk? Where were they?

I took out my sharp knife and started to cut the ship's anchor rope. This was my plan. I wanted to cut through the anchor rope. Then the sea would carry the ship away. The ship would drift onto the shore at another part of the island. Then the pirates would not know where the ship was. They would not be able to leave the island. If I could cut the rope, the ship would drift.

But the rope was very thick. I worked slowly. It took a long time. Slowly the rope came apart.

A gentle wind was blowing and the ship moved. The rope broke. The ship was free of its anchor. The ship began to drift away from the bay.

I heard shouts from the *Hispaniola*. Suddenly I was afraid. Had the men on board seen me? I pulled out one of the pistols which I had in my belt.

No. The men had not seen me. There was the sound of fighting on the ship. I wanted to see what was happening. I still held the anchor rope. The ship was drifting and pulling me along.

I climbed up the rope and looked through a window in the side of the ship. Two men with red faces were fighting in a cabin. They were drunk.

Quickly I climbed back down into Ben Gunn's boat. Now the *Hispaniola* was drifting across the sea. I moved along beside the ship in my small boat.

I tried to paddle back to Treasure Island. But the wind was too strong. It was blowing me away from the island.

At last, I could not paddle any more. I was too tired. I lay down in the small boat and I slept. I dreamt of home and the old Admiral Benbow Inn.

Sunlight woke me up. I saw the *Hispaniola* not far away. It was drifting towards me. My small boat was moving up and down in the water.

The ship moved past me. I paddled towards it. The anchor rope hung down from the back of the ship. I took hold of the rope.

Suddenly the wind blew strongly and the *Hispaniola* turned round. Water came over the sides of my small boat and the boat began to sink. I was still holding the ship's anchor rope. In a few seconds my boat had sunk. I had nowhere else to go. So I pulled myself up onto the deck of the *Hispaniola*.

11

Aboard the *Hispaniola*

There were two men on the deck of the *Hispaniola*. One of them was dead. He had a knife in his chest and he lay in a pool of blood. The other man was sitting near the ship's wheel. His face was white and he was wounded. These were the men I had seen fighting.

The man by the ship's wheel said, 'Rum. Give me a drink of rum.'

I went to the galley and found a bottle of rum. Two more dead pirates were lying in there. I took a drink to the man on the deck.

'Thanks, boy,' said the wounded sailor. 'Where are we heading?'

I looked across the sea. I could see Treasure Island. The ship had drifted north in the night.

'I can see the island,' I said. 'I will steer the *Hispaniola* onto the north shore. The wind is blowing that way. I will run the ship onto the sandy beach.'

I went to the ship's wheel. I had not steered the ship before, but I had seen how it was done. Treasure Island lay ahead. I had to keep the ship moving straight ahead. I tried to keep the ship moving towards the north shore of the island. The pirates were on the south shore of the island. I tried to steer straight for the beach.

All the time the wounded pirate watched me. After a while he came slowly across the deck towards me.

'I'll help you,' he said.

He pointed to a sandy beach in a bay. 'Take the ship into that bay,' he said. 'The water is shallow because the tide is out. The *Hispaniola* will stay on the sand. When the tide comes in the water will get deeper. Then the ship will float off the sand.'

I did as he told me and steered for the beach. I tried to watch him too. The pirate was wounded, but he was still dangerous.

We had almost reached the shore when the pirate stood up. He had a knife in his hand. He moved towards me swinging his knife. I had a pair of pistols in my belt. I took out a pistol and pointed it at him.

'Don't come any closer,' I said, 'or I'll shoot.'

The pirate smiled and moved forward. I closed my eyes and fired the pistol.

Nothing happened.

The pirate laughed and came towards me. I knew he was going to kill me.

At that moment the *Hispaniola* ran onto the beach and stopped suddenly. The pirate and I fell onto the deck.

I jumped up quickly. Where could I run? Where could I hide? There was nowhere to go – except up!

I started to climb the ropes of the mainmast.

The pirate threw his knife, but it did not hit me. I climbed up the mainmast quickly. I was very afraid.

The pirate picked up his knife and started to climb after me. I took out my second pistol and pointed it at him. He laughed. Then he threw the knife. I felt a terrible pain in my left shoulder. The knife had gone through my shoulder and into the mainmast. Hot blood ran down my arm. I fired the pistol. This time there was a loud crack.

The pirate turned slowly and fell into the sea. I had shot him in the chest.

I pulled at the knife which held me to the mast. The wound was not bad. But it was painful and there was a lot of blood.

I climbed back down onto the deck and looked at the island. The ship was not moving. It would stay on the beach without an anchor. I hoped the ship would float again. We needed it to return home.

The *Hispaniola* was no longer a pirate ship. I pulled down the Jolly Roger – the pirate flag.

Now I had to go back to the stockade. I climbed off the ship and onto the beach. I started to walk to the south of the island.

12

The Pirates' Prisoner

It was a long walk. I walked all day. Many times I stopped to rest. At last I came to the place where I had met Ben Gunn. I knew the stockade was close.

The sun went down and night came. I moved forward slowly. I did not want to meet the pirates.

There were no lights in the stockade. I climbed the wall of the stockade carefully and slowly I went towards the cabin.

I fell over a man's leg. I woke someone up. Suddenly, a loud voice came out of the darkness.

'Pieces of eight! Pieces of eight! Pieces of eight!'

'Who's there?' shouted a voice.

It was the voice of Long John Silver.

The pirates were in the stockade! I was their prisoner!

They lit a fire. Then Long John Silver spoke to me. 'Your friends have left you,' he said.

'Where are they?' I asked.

'I don't know,' replied Silver. 'Dr Livesey shouted to me. He said that the ship had gone. He said that they didn't want to fight any more. He made peace with us. Then he and the others left the stockade. They don't want you with them, Jim.'

I did not know what to think. I had left my friends in the stockade. I had not told them where I was going. But did they think I was a friend of the pirates now?

'I don't know if I believe you,' I said to Silver. 'But I know I'm your prisoner.'

'But we're friends, Jim,' he said. 'We're in this together.'

I looked around the stockade. The other pirates had moved away from us. They were talking to each other and looking at Silver and me.

'The men aren't happy,' said Silver. 'There's trouble coming. But I've got the map. Dr Livesey gave me the map. Why did he do that, do you think?'

I did not have time to think. The other pirates came across the stockade towards us. They stood together in front of Silver.

'Me and the lads have been talking,' said one of them.

'Have you?' said Silver.

'Yes,' the other pirate went on. 'And we don't want you as our captain.'

'Do you think it was me who lost the ship?' asked Silver.

'This voyage to find Flint's treasure has been unlucky,' said a pirate.

'Unlucky!' Silver stood up and leant on his crutch. 'Is this unlucky?'

He held up the treasure map in front of the pirates.

'The treasure is no good to us. We've got no ship,' said a pirate.

'There's another ship coming, lads,' said Silver. 'Squire Trelawney chartered a second ship. If he doesn't return in two months, a second ship will come to look for him.'

The men looked at each other. They did not know what to say now.

'The first thing we'll do is get the treasure,' said Silver. 'We'll go and find it early tomorrow morning.'

The men went away and talked together. They seemed happy now. Soon they lay down and went to sleep. Silver and I did the same.

In the morning we heard Dr Livesey's voice. 'Silver, I've come to see the wounded men, as we agreed,' he said.

When he saw me, Dr Livesey was surprised.

'Jim! What are you doing here?' he said.

I looked at Silver. 'I must speak to the Doctor,' I said.

'Be careful, Jim,' said Silver. 'You're with me now, remember.'

What did the Doctor think of me? I had left him and my friends in the stockade. I walked slowly to the Doctor.

'Where did you go?' asked the Doctor in a quiet voice.

'I went to the *Hispaniola*,' I whispered quickly. 'The ship is at the north end of the island.'

The Doctor went and looked at the wounded pirates. Then he got ready to go. But before he left, he whispered to me, 'I've found Ben Gunn.'

13

The Search for the Treasure

After Dr Livesey had left, I ate breakfast with the pirates.

'We'll get that treasure, lads,' Silver said to the pirates. 'We'll each have some of that treasure. We'll share it out among us. Now, let's go.'

We all went off to find the treasure. The men carried picks and shovels to dig it up. Silver and I walked in front of the men.

'You'll not try to run away, will you, Jim?' asked Silver.

But, before I could answer, he put a rope round my neck. He pulled me along like a dog.

Silver looked at the treasure map. He read out the directions.

'Tall tree. Spy-Glass Hill. North by north-east. Ten feet.'

So we were looking for a tall tree on Spy-Glass Hill. We knew the hill was the highest part of the island.

It was not a long walk, but the hill was very steep. By midday we were tired. We rested before we climbed to the top of Spy-Glass Hill.

One of the pirates walked a little way ahead of us. Suddenly he shouted out – 'Look, lads, here!'

We all ran forward.

'Have you found the treasure?' one pirate asked.

We came round some bushes and saw white bones. A skeleton of a man lay on the ground. Its bony fingers pointed up the hill.

'It's one of Flint's men,' said Silver. 'It's one of the men that helped him bury the treasure.'

'Aye,' said another pirate. 'Flint took six men with him to bury the treasure. But only Flint came back. Flint killed them all.'

'And Flint's dead,' said Silver. 'He can't hurt you now. Come on. We're nearly at the top of the hill.'

The other pirates looked at each other. They were afraid. But they went on walking up the hill.

We rested again before the top of the hill. Up ahead we could see three tall trees. One tree stood higher than the rest.

'That's the tree,' said a pirate. 'We'll find the treasure near it.'

'The treasure is ours,' said another pirate. 'Let's dig it up.'

'Let's stop and eat first,' said Silver. 'Digging up treasure is hard work.'

'I don't want to stop here,' said a pirate. 'This is Flint's place. And Flint was an evil man.'

'He's dead,' said Silver.

The men spoke in quiet voices. They looked around them. They were afraid.

Suddenly we heard a strange, high voice. It sang the pirate song.

Fifteen men on the dead man's chest -
Yo-ho-ho and a bottle of rum!

The pirates were very frightened now. Their faces went white.

'It's Flint!' cried one of them.

'He's come to kill us!' cried another.

'I know that voice,' said Silver. 'It's not Flint's voice. Come on. Let's go and see.'

The other pirates would not move.

'It's Flint, I tell you. We're all going to die.'

'It's not Flint,' said Silver. 'I know that voice – it's Ben Gunn!'

Silver pulled at the rope round my neck. We went up to the top of the hill.

'Seven hundred thousand pounds in gold,' said Silver. 'It's here. I know it's here.'

He pulled at my rope. The other pirates ran forward. They shouted to each other. Then they stopped.

Near the tall tree was a big hole in the ground. It was a wide, deep hole. I knew at once that the treasure had been buried here. But the hole was empty.

The pirates jumped into the hole. They started digging with their picks and shovels. Silver stood beside me at the edge of the hole. He gave me a pistol.

Near the tall tree was a big hole in the ground. But the hole was empty.

'Here, take this pistol, Jim,' he said. 'There's trouble coming. Watch out.'

One of the pirates found two gold coins. He held them up for everyone to see.

'I've found two gold coins,' he shouted at Silver. 'Two gold coins! Where's the seven hundred thousand pounds? Where's Flint's treasure?'

The pirates jumped out of the hole. They stood in front of us. They were mad with anger.

'We'll kill you,' shouted one of them. 'Come on, lads. Kill them both. Kill the liar with one leg. Kill the boy too.'

Silver and I aimed our pistols at the pirates. Just then, three musket shots cracked out from the trees. Two of the pirates fell to the ground. Silver fired his pistol. The other pirates ran away.

Dr Livesey, Squire Trelawney and Ben Gunn came out of the trees. They held muskets in their hands.

'Thank you, Doctor,' Silver said to Dr Livesey. 'You came at the right time.'

'Come quickly,' said the Doctor. 'The pirates will come back. We must take their boats. We must get back to the *Hispaniola*.'

We walked back to the beach near the stockade as quickly as we could. As we walked, Dr Livesey told us the story of the treasure.

'Ben Gunn found Flint's treasure while he was alone on the island. He dug it up. The treasure was in a large chest. Ben Gunn took the treasure out of the chest. He carried it to the north of the island. It took a long time. The treasure is safe in a cave now.'

14
Flint's Treasure

We went to the boats near the stockade. Then we rowed round to the north of the island. The sun went down into the sea. It had been a long day and I was very tired.

Captain Smollett had floated the *Hispaniola* off the beach at high tide. He had anchored the ship again in the deep water of the north bay.

We all went to Ben Gunn's cave. We made a big fire and cooked a meal. The bright light of the fire shone on hundreds of gold coins. The gold coins were Captain Flint's treasure.

'So, that is Flint's treasure,' said Long John Silver. 'Seven hundred thousand pounds. Many men have died for that money.'

I was silent. I stared at the gold. Yes, men had died for the money. Silver had killed some of them himself.

The next day we began to carry the gold to the *Hispaniola*. There were Spanish pieces of eight and also English, French and Portuguese coins.

Day after day, the work went on. We watched for the pirates, but we did not see them.

There was food and drink at the stockade. We also left food at Ben Gunn's cave. We were going to leave the pirates on the island. But they would have plenty of food. As soon as all the gold was loaded on the ship, we left the island. We were a small crew and everyone had to work very hard. Silver cooked the food in the galley. He had brought his parrot back from the stockade. The parrot sat in its cage in the galley.

The bright light of the fire shone on hundreds of gold coins.
The gold coins were Captain Flint's treasure.

'Pieces of eight! Pieces of eight!' screamed the parrot.

We sailed the ship round to the south of the island. We saw three pirates standing on the beach. We sailed as close to them as we could.

'Don't leave us!' cried the pirates. 'Don't leave us here to die!'

Dr Livesey called to them. He told them about Ben Gunn's cave. He told them there was food in the cave and in the stockade.

We sailed north into the Gulf of Mexico. When we reached land, we anchored the ship. There were many trees growing near the coast. Small boats came out from the shore and the Indians brought us fruit and water.

There was an English ship nearby. Captain Smollett, Squire Trelawney, Dr Livesey and I rowed over to the ship in one of the small boats. We told our story to the ship's captain.

When we returned to the *Hispaniola*, Silver was gone. He had taken the other small boat and three thousand pounds. He was a pirate, a murderer and thief. But I had liked the man.

We never saw or heard of him again.

———

In England we shared the treasure. We each had some of the money. Captain Smollett bought himself a house on the coast. From there he could see ships sailing to all parts of the world. Squire Trelawney was now a very rich man. He went back to live in the big white house on the hill. Dr Livesey became a wealthy doctor in London. Ben Gunn spent his money in three weeks and became a beggar.

My mother and I bought a fine, large inn and had many servants. The rest of my money paid for me to study.

I did not want any more adventures. I did not want to go to sea again. But I wanted to write about my adventures. And now you have read my story.

———

Sometimes I wake up at night. I can hear the sea around Treasure Island. I can hear the voice of Long John Silver's parrot, Captain Flint, calling – 'Pieces of eight! Pieces of eight! Pieces of eight!'

Points for Understanding

1

1 Where do Jim Hawkins and his parents live?
2 Who is the stranger who comes to stay with Jim Hawkins?
  What does he bring with him?
3 A second stranger arrives. Why does he come?

2

1 The Captain tells Jim that Flint's men are looking for him.
  What do they want?
2 What does Blind Pew do when he comes to the Admiral
  Benbow Inn?
3 Why do Jim and his mother run to the village?
4 What do Jim and his mother find in the Captain's sea-chest?
5 How does Blind Pew die?

3

1 Dr Livesey and Squire John Trelawney find something in a
  leather packet. What is it?
2 What does Squire Trelawney decide to do?

4

1 Squire Trelawney charters a ship in Bristol. What is the
  name of the ship? How many sailors does Trelawney hire?
  What is the name of the captain of the ship?
2 What do you learn about Long John Silver in this chapter?
3 What is Jim Hawkins' job on the ship?
4 Who says, 'Pieces of eight. Pieces of eight'?

5

1 I woke up when I heard voices.
  (a)   Where is Jim?
  (b)   Who is talking?
  (c)   What are the voices talking about?

2 The *Hispaniola* arrives at the island. What does Jim do next?

6

1 How does Jim know about Spy-Glass Hill and the stockade before he goes to the island?
2 How many men go with Silver to the island?
3 What does Jim do?
4 What does Jim see Long John Silver do on the island?

7

1 Who does Jim meet on the island?
2 What do you learn about this person?

8

1 Who tells this part of the story?
2 How many men go with Captain Smollett, Squire Trelawney and Dr Livesey to the island?
3 Why does their boat sink?
4 What happens when they get to the stockade?

9

1 Long John Silver comes to the stockade with a white flag. Why does he do this?
2 What happens after Long John Silver leaves the stockade?
3 What does Jim do after it gets dark?

10

1 How does Jim get to the *Hispaniola*?
2 What is Jim's plan?
3 Jim climbs up a rope and looks through a window in the side of the *Hispaniola*. What does he see?
4 Jim falls asleep. What happens when he wakes up the next morning?

11

1 The wounded pirate says, 'Take the ship into that bay.'
   Why does the pirate tell Jim to do this?
2 The pirate wounds Jim in the shoulder. How does the pirate
   do this?
3 What happens when Jim fires the second pistol?

12

1 When he gets back to the stockade, Jim gets a surprise.
   Why?
2 The men went away and talked together. They seemed
   happy now. Why do the men seem happy now?
3 Why does Dr Livesey come to the stockade?
4 What does Jim tell Dr Livesey? What does Dr Livesey tell
   Jim?

13

1 How does Silver stop Jim running away?
2 While the pirates are climbing Spy-Glass Hill:
   (a)   What do they see?
   (b)   What do they hear?
3 What do the pirates find at the top of Spy-Glass Hill?
4 Who stops the pirates from killing Long John Silver and
   Jim?

14

1 Where is Flint's treasure?
2 What is Flint's treasure?
3 What happens to each of these people?
   (a)   Long John Silver
   (b)   Captain Smollett
   (c)   Dr Livesey
   (d)   Ben Gunn
   (e)   Jim Hawkins

ELEMENTARY LEVEL

A Christmas Carol *by Charles Dickens*
Riders of the Purple Sage *by Zane Grey*
The Canterville Ghost and Other Stories *by Oscar Wilde*
Lady Portia's Revenge and Other Stories *by David Evans*
The Picture of Dorian Gray *by Oscar Wilde*
Treasure Island *by Robert Louis Stevenson*
Road to Nowhere *by John Milne*
The Black Cat *by John Milne*
Don't Tell Me What To Do *by Michael Hardcastle*
The Runaways *by Victor Canning*
The Red Pony *by John Steinbeck*
The Goalkeeper's Revenge and Other Stories *by Bill Naughton*
The Stranger *by Norman Whitney*
The Promise *by R. L. Scott-Buccleuch*
The Man With No Name *by Evelyn Davies and Peter Town*
The Cleverest Person in the World *by Norman Whitney*
Claws *by John Landon*
Z for Zachariah *by Robert C. O'Brien*
Tales of Horror *by Bram Stoker*
Frankenstein *by Mary Shelley*
Silver Blaze and Other Stories *by Sir Arthur Conan Doyle*
Tales of Ten Worlds *by Arthur C. Clarke*
The Boy Who Was Afraid *by Armstrong Sperry*
Room 13 and Other Ghost Stories *by M. R. James*
The Narrow Path *by Francis Selormey*
The Woman in Black *by Susan Hill*

For further information on the full selection of
Readers at all five levels in the series, please refer
to the Macmillan Readers catalogue.

Published by Macmillan Heinemann ELT
Between Towns Road, Oxford OX4 3PP
Macmillan Heinemann ELT is an imprint of
Macmillan Publishers Limited
Companies and representatives throughout the world

ISBN 0 435 27214 4

This retold version by Stephen Colbourn for Macmillan Guided Readers
First published 1993
Text © Stephen Colbourn 1993, 1998, 2002
Design and illustration © Macmillan Publishers Limited 1998, 2002
Heinemann is a registered trademark of Reed Educational & Professional Publishing Limited
This version first published 2002

Illustrated by Victor Ambrus
Cover by Robert Andrew and Threefold Design

Printed in China

2006 2005 2004 2003 2002
16 15 14 13 12 11 10 9